Date: 8/6/12

J 636.73 GOL
Goldish, Meish.
Rottweiler : super courageous

BIG DOGS RULE

Rottweiler
Super Courageous

by Meish Goldish

Consultant: Elaine Starry
Rottweiler Breeder
www.andelrottweilers.com

BEARPORT
PUBLISHING

New York, New York

Credits

Cover and Title Page, © Degtyaryov Andrey Leonidovich/Shutterstock; TOC, © FotoJagodka/Shutterstock; 4, © Sam Furlong/SWNS.com; 5, © Jeannie Harrison/Close Encounters of the Furry Kind; 6, © www.rspcaphotolibrary.com; 7, © www.rspcaphotolibrary.com; 9, Courtesy of Donautalbahner; 10, © Photo by Robert Rosamilio/NY Daily News Archive via Getty Images; 11, © Marka/SuperStock; 12, © Patricia Vazquez/SuperStock; 13, © John Daniels/Ardea; 14, © Fritz Clark/The Standard Image; 15, © Jeannie Harrison/Close Encounters of the Furry Kind; 16, © Featurechina/George Ng/Newscom; 17, © Ken Love/Newscom; 18, © Jeannie Harrison/Close Encounters of the Furry Kind; 19L, © R. Richter/Tierfotoagentur/Alamy; 19TR, © Arco Images GmbH/Photolibrary; 19BR, © Andreas Marinski/age fotostock; 20, © bonzami Emmanuelle/Pixmac; 21, Porteous Gregg © Newspix/News Ltd/3rd Party Managed Reproduction & Supply Rights; 22, © John Daniels/Ardea; 23, © Stephen Coburn/Shutterstock; 24, © Bianca Lagalla/Shutterstock; 25, © Minden Pictures/SuperStock; 26, © Wales News Service; 27, © Wales News Service; 28, © Ian Mckenzie; 29T, © FotoJagodka/Shutterstock; 29B, © Elaine Starry/ANDEL Rottweilers; 31, © Linn Currie/Shutterstock.

Publisher: Kenn Goin
Editorial Director: Adam Siegel
Creative Director: Spencer Brinker
Design: Dawn Beard Creative
Cover Design: Dawn Beard Creative and Kim Jones
Photo Researcher: Mary Fran Loftus

Library of Congress Cataloging-in-Publication Data

Goldish, Meish.
  Rottweiler : super courageous / by Meish Goldish.
    p. cm. — (Big dogs rule)
  Includes bibliographical references and index.
  ISBN-13: 978-1-61772-298-1 (library binding)
  ISBN-10: 1-61772-298-7 (library binding)
  1. Rottweiler dog—Juvenile literature. I. Title.
  SF429.R7G65 2012
  636.73—dc22
                  2011015914

For more information, write to Bearport Publishing Company, Inc., 45 West 21st Street, Suite 3B, New York, New York 10010. Printed in the United States of America in North Mankato, Minnesota.

071511
042711CGD

10 9 8 7 6 5 4 3 2 1

Contents

Jake to the Rescue

One evening in 2009, Liz Maxted-Bluck of Coventry, England, was strolling through the park. Alongside her was Jake, her two-year-old Rottweiler (ROT-*wye*-lur). Suddenly, the two of them heard a woman screaming in the distance. The large dog leaped into action, racing into the nearby woods where the sounds were coming from.

Liz Maxted-Bluck with her Rottweiler, Jake

Liz ran to catch up with her dog. As she did, Liz saw a man rush out of the woods. He looked terrified because the big, powerful Rottweiler was running after him. After chasing the man away, Jake returned to Liz and led her to the woman who had been attacked. Liz immediately phoned the police.

Rottweilers have a natural desire, or **instinct**, to protect people and property when they sense danger.

A Big Honor

Jake guarded the attack victim until the police arrived. Luckily, the officers were able to find and catch the attacker within a few hours. They praised the Rottweiler for his **courageous** deed. The following year, Jake was honored by the Royal Society for the Prevention of Cruelty to Animals (RSPCA). The organization gave the dog a special medal for his bravery.

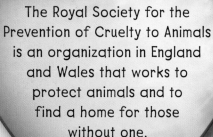

Jake proudly wears ▶ the medal awarded to him by the RSPCA.

The Royal Society for the Prevention of Cruelty to Animals is an organization in England and Wales that works to protect animals and to find a home for those without one.

No one was prouder of Jake's award than his owners, Liz and her husband, Ian. Liz said, "It is especially touching because we got Jake from the RSPCA." She had adopted the Rottweiler in 2008 after finding him in an RSPCA **animal shelter**. Liz added, "I always feel safe when I'm out walking with him."

▲ **Jake with his owners, Ian and Liz**

Dogs at Work

Jake was a hero, but his bravery was hardly surprising. For a long time, Rottweilers have shown that they can quickly take charge of tough situations. Back in the 1100s, butchers in the large, busy town of Rottweil, Germany, went to distant places to buy cattle. They needed to **herd** the animals back to their town. The dogs they used for the job became known as Rottweilers. They were also the **ancestors** of today's Rottweilers.

Hundreds of years ago, Rottweilers worked for butchers in the busy market town of Rottweil, Germany. At that time, the animals were also called "the butcher's dog of Rottweil."

GERMANY

•Rottweil

According to **legend,** a Rottweiler that herded cattle for a butcher would carry its owner's money in a purse around its neck. No one dared to steal from the powerful dog!

Often, two Rottweilers were used to guide a long line of cattle along a road. Each dog worked on one side of the group. If a cow tried to break free and run away, the Rottweiler stepped in. The dog was much smaller than the cow. However, one angry look from the tough-looking Rottweiler was usually enough to keep the huge animal in line.

Rottweil was a center of trade for the buying and selling of farm goods and cattle. Today, this statue honoring Rottweilers stands in front of a museum in the town.

Changing Jobs

By the 1850s, Rottweilers were no longer needed to help **transport** cattle. That's because the newly invented railroad car did the job instead. For about 50 years, people had no special use for Rottweilers. Then, in the early 1900s, people in Germany found a new job for the big, powerful **canines**. Rottweilers became police dogs. They were trained to work with police officers and follow their **commands**.

▲ Rottweilers continue to make good police dogs because they are strong, quick, intelligent, and brave.

During World War I (1914–1918) and World War II (1939–1945), Rottweilers also served in the German army. Some were patrol dogs trained to hunt for enemy troops on the battlefield. Others were used to guard captured soldiers in German **prisoner-of-war camps**.

During wartime, some Rottweilers were trained to deliver secret messages in tubes attached to their collars. The dogs were usually successful because they could travel quickly and quietly across a battlefield.

◀ **Today, Rottweilers still work with soldiers. This dog, for example, is trained to find bombs.**

Welcome to America

For hundreds of years, Rottweilers were important working dogs in Germany. However, there weren't any in America until 1928. That year, some German **immigrants** came to the United States with their Rottweilers. Soon they began to **breed** the dogs. In 1930, the first **litter** of Rottweiler pups was born in America. Rottweilers were now being raised in the United States.

Today, Rottweilers are bred throughout the United States—and around the world.

At first, few Americans showed an interest in them. That changed in the mid-1980s, when more people wanted guard dogs to protect their homes and families. Suddenly, the Rottweiler was a big dog in big demand.

▼ **By the 1990s, Rottweilers were the most popular dogs in the United States after Labrador retrievers.**

According to records kept by the **American Kennel Club,** there were only about 13,000 Rottweilers in the United States in 1983. By 1994, the number had soared to more than 100,000.

How Big Is Big?

The American Kennel Club (AKC) keeps records of the different kinds of dogs bred in the United States. For each breed of dog, the AKC writes a **standard**. This detailed description explains how the **ideal** dog of the breed should look and behave.

It is difficult for a Rottweiler to win points at a **dog show** if it fails to meet the AKC standard.

▲ In dog shows, Rottweilers compete against other Rottweilers, as well as against dogs of other breeds.

The AKC standard for the Rottweiler describes the dog as "medium large" in size. How big is that, exactly? According to the AKC, a male Rottweiler should be no shorter than 24 inches (61 cm) and no taller than 27 inches (69 cm) at the shoulder. A female should be between 22 and 25 inches (56 to 64 cm) tall at the shoulder.

A male Rottweiler (left) is slightly larger than a female (right).

Happy to Help

In its official description of Rottweilers, the AKC writes that "the Rottweiler is happiest when given a job to perform." Today, these hardworking dogs help people in a variety of ways. Some work on farms as animal herders, just as they did hundreds of years ago. Others continue to serve as police dogs.

These Rottweilers ▶ work with police officers in China.

In addition, Rottweilers have two newer jobs. Some are **service dogs** that help **disabled** people, such as those in wheelchairs. Tasks the dogs learn include opening and closing doors and picking up items that a person has dropped.

Rottweilers also get to show off their caring, helpful side when they work as **therapy dogs**, visiting people in hospitals and nursing homes. There, the big dogs' gentleness and calmness make them pleasant company and help cheer up people.

Many kinds of dogs, including Rottweilers, work as therapy dogs. The dogs receive special testing and training to make sure they will get along well with everyone they meet.

Fun-Loving Pets

Rottweilers are hardworking animals. Yet they are also gentle and playful. As a result, they've become popular household pets. They are loyal and **affectionate** and like to cuddle with humans. In addition to keeping family members safe, the dogs are happy to keep their owners company as they make dinner, do their homework, or watch television.

A Rottweiler's smooth, shiny coat is easy to **groom**. It just needs a firm brushing and a washing if the dog gets into mud or dirt.

When they are not relaxing around the house, pet Rottweilers need to get lots of exercise. The big, **rugged** dogs enjoy walking, running, and playing. They can spend hours **retrieving** a ball or catching a flying disc—or playing any other game that allows them to have fun with their families.

▲ **Rottweilers often look thoughtful and serious, but they have their fun side, too.**

Living Together

Rottweilers that live with people as pets usually get along well with both adults and children. However, there are some important rules that families who own or are thinking of owning the big dogs need to keep in mind.

For example, children need to learn to be gentle around Rottweilers. A child who hugs one too tightly or pulls too hard on its ears might upset or startle the big dog and suddenly get knocked over.

Children who are gentle with Rottweilers find that the dogs are gentle in return.

Rottweilers also demand a lot of attention from their owners. They don't like to be left alone in a room or yard. If they feel ignored, they may become restless and damage property. Owners who spend lots of time with their big friends will receive lots of love in return.

Rottweiler owners must be calm but firm when training their dogs. Because Rottweilers have strong, take-charge personalities, a Rottweiler that is not well trained may try to take over the household.

▲ **Rottweilers like a lot of attention.**

Pups Growing Up

Although Rottweilers grow up to be big dogs, they start out very small. At birth, a Rottweiler weighs only around one pound (.45 kg)—about as much as a football. Usually, there are 8 to 12 puppies born in a litter.

▼ **Rottweilers are born with their eyes closed. They don't open them until they are about two weeks old.**

Newborn Rottweilers start out by drinking their mother's milk. The puppies grow quickly. Within eight or nine days, their weight usually doubles. Then, when they are about four weeks old, they start eating solid food called puppy chow. Most of the time the dogs reach their full height by the age of 12 months. Fully grown, a Rottweiler weighs around 100 pounds (45 kg)—or about as much as the average 13-year-old child.

Dog experts advise people not to bring home Rottweiler pups before the dogs are eight weeks old. By that time, they are ready to leave their mother and live with a human family.

▲ **Rottweiler pups drinking their mother's milk**

The Great Debate

In recent years, Rottweilers have been the subject of a heated **debate**. Some people claim that the dogs are **vicious**. They point to cases where Rottweilers have bitten, injured, and even killed people. As a result, some towns in the United States have passed laws against owning a Rottweiler.

Like owners of other dog breeds, Rottweiler owners say that training the dog from a young age is very important in order to make sure it becomes a well-behaved adult.

Rottweiler owners, however, insist that their dogs are not dangerous. They claim the canines are completely safe—as long as they're bred, raised, and trained properly. The problem, they say, is that some owners encourage their animals to be vicious. "There's no such thing as a bad dog," they argue, "just a bad owner."

The AKC runs a program in which Rottweilers and other dogs can earn a Canine Good Citizen certificate. Dogs who pass the tests within the program prove that they have good manners around all kinds of people, including strangers.

▲ Rottweilers are usually quick to learn, so they respond well to good training.

Doggone Love

Rottweilers are known for being hardworking and loyal dogs—but they are also very loving and caring. In 2009, an English pig breeder named Heidi Rhiann had a serious problem. One of her newborn pigs, named Apple Sauce, was being ignored by its mother because it was the **runt** of the litter. Without its mother's milk, the **piglet** would soon starve to death.

Pigs, like dogs, feed only on their mother's milk for the first few weeks of their lives.

▲ **Heidi with her pet Rottweiler and Apple Sauce**

Heidi had an idea. She placed the piglet into a new litter of Rottweiler pups. Heidi hoped that the mother Rottweiler would **nurse** the helpless runt. Luckily, she did! The dog fed the tiny pig, which grew stronger and healthier. The surprising event proved once again that Rottweilers are big dogs with big, loving hearts.

▼ **Apple Sauce sleeps with her new family—a litter of Rottweilers.**

Rottweilers at a Glance

Weight:	Male: 95 to 130 pounds (43 to 59 kg) Female: 85 to 115 pounds (39 to 52 kg)
Height at Shoulder:	Male: 24 to 27 inches (61 to 69 cm) Female: 22 to 25 inches (56 to 64 cm)
Coat:	Straight and coarse medium-length hair that lies flat
Colors:	Black with mahogany (reddish-brown) markings
Country of Origin:	Germany
Life Span:	About 10 to 12 years
Personality:	Intelligent, brave, hardworking, playful, loving, protective; likes plenty of attention from its owners

Best in Show

What makes a great Rottweiler? Every owner knows that his or her dog is special. Judges in dog shows, however, look very carefully at a Rottweiler's appearance and behavior. Here are some of the things they look for:

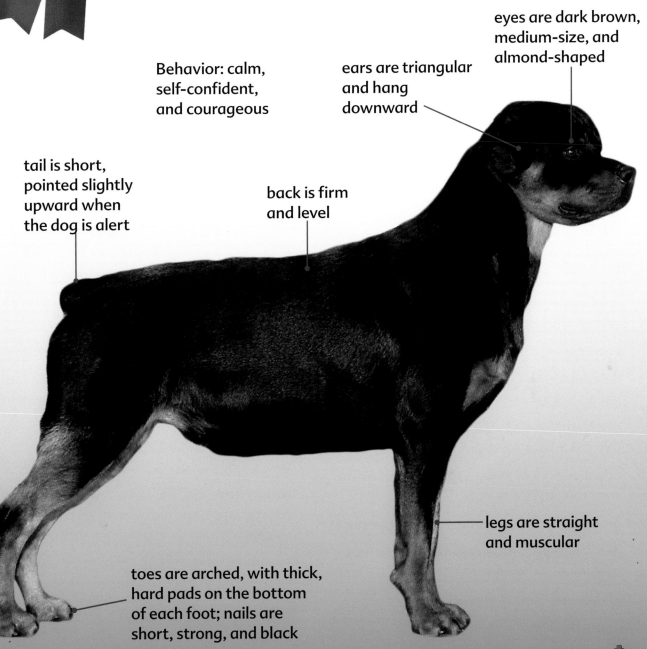

eyes are dark brown, medium-size, and almond-shaped

ears are triangular and hang downward

Behavior: calm, self-confident, and courageous

tail is short, pointed slightly upward when the dog is alert

back is firm and level

legs are straight and muscular

toes are arched, with thick, hard pads on the bottom of each foot; nails are short, strong, and black

Glossary

affectionate (uh-FEK-shuh-nuht) friendly and loving

American Kennel Club (uh-MER-i-kuhn KEN-uhl KLUHB) a national organization that is involved with many activities having to do with dogs, including collecting information about dog breeds and setting rules for dog shows

ancestors (AN-sess-turz) members of a family or group who lived a long time ago

animal shelter (AN-uh-muhl SHEL-tur) a place where homeless animals can stay until they find a new home

breed (BREED) to keep animals with special characteristics so that they can mate and produce offspring with those same characteristics

canines (KAY-nyenz) members of the dog family

commands (kuh-MANDZ) orders given to a person or animal

courageous (kuh-RAY-juhss) brave

debate (di-BAYT) a discussion of a problem or issue

disabled (diss-AY-buhld) unable to do certain things due to an injury or illness

dog show (DAWG SHOH) a gathering where dogs compete for awards

groom (GROOM) to brush and clean an animal

herd (HURD) to make animals move together as a group

ideal (eye-DEE-uhl) perfect; just right

immigrants (IM-uh-gruhnts) people who come from one country to live in a new one

instinct (IN-stingkt) knowledge and ways of acting that an animal is born with

legend (LEJ-uhnd) a story handed down from long ago that is often based on some facts but cannot be proven true

litter (LIT-ur) a group of baby animals, such as puppies or kittens, that are born to the same mother at the same time

nurse (NURSS) to feed a young animal milk that comes from its mother

piglet (PIG-lit) a baby pig

prisoner-of-war camps (*priz*-uhn-ur-uhv-WOR KAMPS) places where soldiers captured during wartime are held and guarded by the enemy

retrieving (ri-TREE-ving) getting or bringing something back

rugged (RUG-id) strong and tough

runt (RUHNT) the smallest animal of a litter

service dogs (SUR-viss DAWGZ) dogs that are trained to help disabled people, such as those in wheelchairs

standard (STAN-durd) a description of the "perfect" dog in each breed

therapy dogs (THER-uh-pee DAWGZ) dogs that visit places such as hospitals to cheer up people and make them feel more comfortable

transport (transs-PORT) to move people or goods from one place to another

vicious (VISH-uhss) fierce and dangerous

Bibliography

Clemente, Victor. *Rottweiler (Breeders' Best).* Allenhurst, NJ: Kennel Club Books (2004).

Holowinski, Margaret. *The Everything Rottweiler Book: A Complete Guide to Raising, Training, and Caring for Your Rottweiler.* Avon, MA: Adams Media (2004).

Kern, Kerry. *Rottweilers (A Complete Pet Owner's Manual).* Hauppauge, NY: Barron's (2009).

Libby, Tracy. *The Rottweiler.* Neptune City, NJ: T.F.H. Publications (2006).

Read More

Fiedler, Julie. *Rottweilers (Tough Dogs).* New York: Rosen (2006).

Gray, Susan H. *Rottweilers (Domestic Dogs).* Mankato, MN: Child's World (2008).

Stone, Lynn M. *Rottweilers (Eye to Eye with Dogs).* Vero Beach, FL: Rourke (2005).

Learn More Online

To learn more about Rottweilers, visit
www.bearportpublishing.com/BigDogsRule

Index

About the Author

Meish Goldish has written more than 200 books for children. His books *Bug-a-licious* and *Michael Phelps: Anything Is Possible!* were Children's Choices Reading List Selections in 2010. He lives in Brooklyn, New York.